My first journey into the Bible
BIBLICAL
A B C

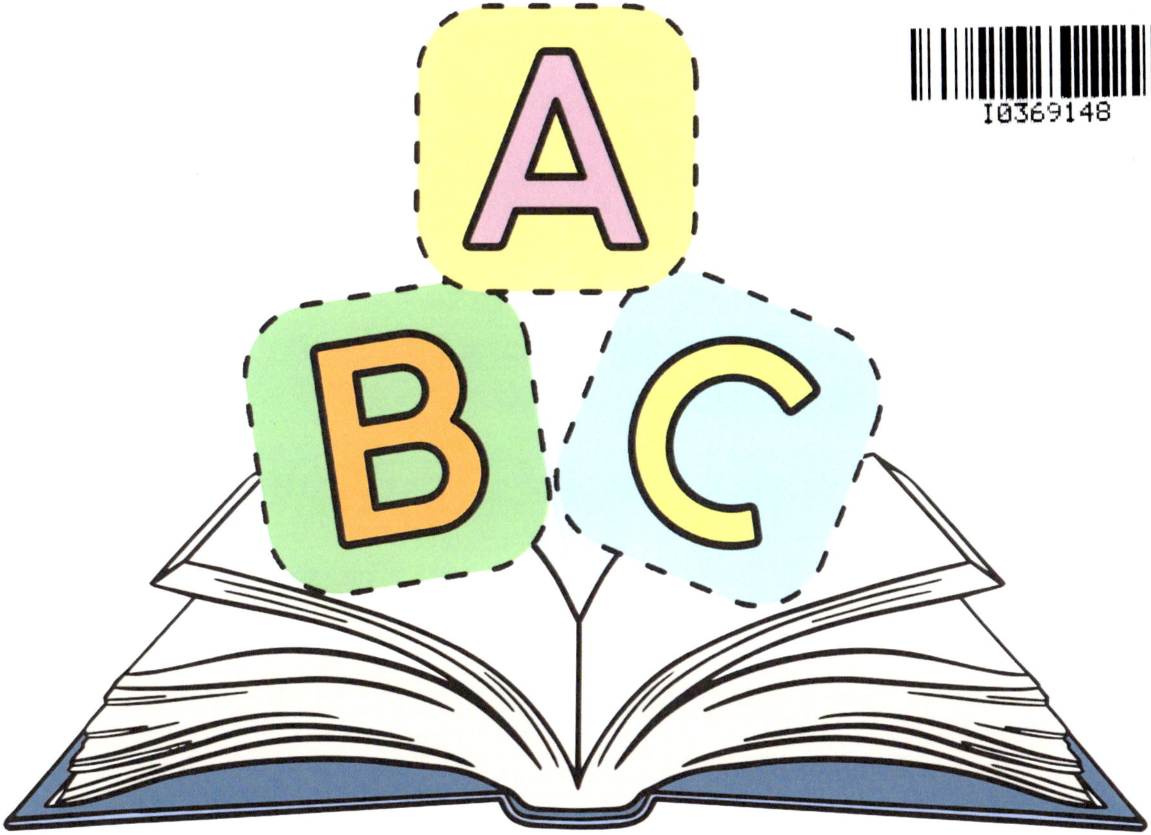

Caroline Khouri

© Caroline Khouri 2023

All rights reserved. No part of this book may be reproduced or transmitted in any form
or by any means, electronic or mechanical, including photocopying, recording, uploading to the internet, or by any information storage and retrieval system, without written permission from the publisher.

Published by Parousia Media Pty Ltd
PO Box 59 Galston, New South Wales, 2159
+61 2 8776 8778
www.parousiamedia.com

ISBN: 978-1-923131-29-3

Printed in Australia

Aa

Genesis 6-9

is for ark

God told Noah to build an **ark** to save his family and two of every animal from the Great Flood.

Bb
is for Bible

The **Bible** tells us stories about God and the life of Jesus.

Luke 22:14-20

is for communion

During Mass, we join together for **communion** to receive the body and blood of Jesus.

Dd

Matthew 10: 2-5

is for disciple

Jesus had 12 **disciples** who followed him and spread his teachings everywhere they went.

Ee

Genesis 1:1

is for Earth

God created the Heavens and the **Earth**.

Matthew 15:32-39

Ff
is for fish

Jesus shared **fish** and bread with those who were hungry.

Gg
is for God

Genesis 1:26-28

God created man, woman and every living creature.

Matthew 9:2-8

Hh
is for heal

Jesus performed miracles and would **heal** those who were sick.

Ii
is for inn

Luke 2:1-7

Mary gave birth to Jesus in a manger because there was no room in the **inn**.

Jj

Mark 6:3

is for Joseph

Jesus was a carpenter just like his earthly father **Joseph**.

Kk

Matthew 13:44

is for Kingdom

The **Kingdom** of Heaven is the greatest gift from God.

Ll
is for love

John 13:34-35

Jesus teaches us to always **love** one another.

Mm

Matthew 1:18

is for Mary

Mary is the mother of Jesus. She is brave and loves Jesus with all of her heart.

Nn
is for Nazareth

Matthew 2:23

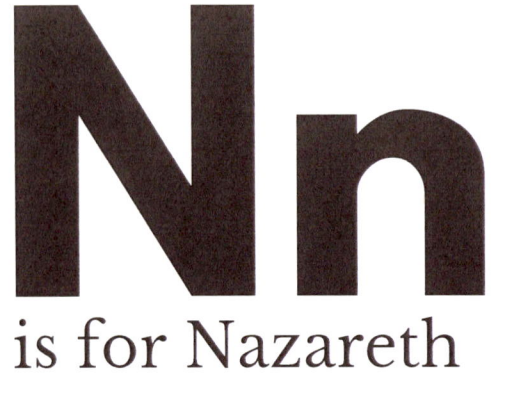

Jesus was born in Bethlehem and grew up in a small town called **Nazareth**.

Oo

is for old

The Bible is divided into two main parts, the **Old** Testament and the New Testament.

Pp

James 5:16

is for pray

We **pray** together as a family every night before we go to bed.

Qq

Revelation 12:1

is for queen

Mary is crowned as the **queen** of Heaven and Earth.

Luke 6:35

Rr
is for reward

God will **reward** us
when we are good to others.

Ss

is for steward

Genesis 1:26

We are **stewards** of the Earth,
which means we need to keep it clean
and safe for others.

Tt

is for teacher

Matthew 22:36-40

Jesus is a **teacher** who shared many important lessons with everyone.

Uu

is for unite

Hebrews 13:16

We can **unite** together to help the sick, the poor and the lonely in our world.

is for vineyard

The workers spent the day in the **vineyard** collecting grapes to make wine.

Ww

Luke 22:14-20

is for wine

At the Last Supper, Jesus broke
bread and shared **wine** with his disciples.

Xx

DID YOU KNOW THAT THERE ARE NO WORDS IN THE BIBLE THAT START WITH THE LETTER 'X'.

Crucifix ends with the letter 'X'.
A crucifix is a cross with Jesus.

Yy

is for you

John 15:9

Jesus is always in your heart.
He loves **you** very much!

Zz
is for zeal

Acts 2:1-12

Zeal is passion. The disciples had great **zeal** after Pentecost.

www.ingramcontent.com/pod-product-compliance
Lightning Source LLC
Chambersburg PA
CBRC100225100526
44591CB00007B/62